Holly Juckes.

Sheila McCullagh and Lois Myers

The Canadian Arctic- on the edge of the frozen sea

GW00701597

Longman

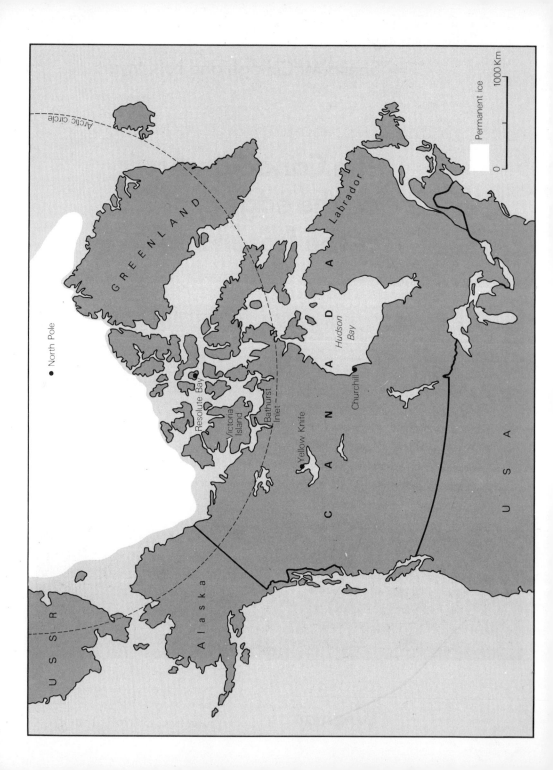

If you live in the northern half of the world,
and look up into the sky at night, you will see a group
of stars called The Great Bear. The name was given
to them by the Greeks, thousands of years ago.

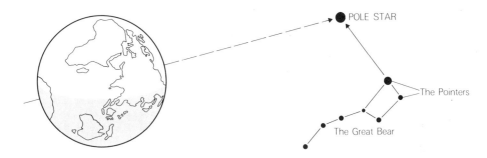

Two of the stars are called 'the pointers',
because they point to the North Star, which is also
called the Pole Star. If you face towards it,
you will be looking towards the North Pole. Our name
for the far north of the world, the Arctic, comes
from the Greek word 'arktos', meaning a bear.

The most northerly point in the world,
the North Pole, is not on land at all. It is ice,
and the ice rests on the Arctic Ocean.
The frozen sea stretches across the top of the world.
The islands and the northern coasts of the great
continents surround the Arctic Ocean. They, too,
are covered in snow and ice for the greater part
of the year.

Nothing grows in the polar desert, but as you
travel south from the pole, you first reach islands
and then the mainland. It is bitterly cold on
the land in winter, but in summer the snow and
ice melt, and flowers and plants can grow.

The coast of Labrador

In northern Canada early in May, the land is still snow-covered, and the sea looks white with broken ice.

The picture below shows the sea still frozen at Resolute Bay in July, although the land is bare of snow.

Summer in the Canadian Arctic is very short. It is only possible to take supplies by ship to the islands off Canada's north coast for about six weeks in late July and August. Then the sea freezes again.

Along the west shore of Hudson Bay

When the snow melts, it leaves behind a land
with thousands of small lakes.

Trees cannot grow in the far north. If you dig
down only a metre – less in some places – you come
to ground which is always frozen. It is called
'the permafrost'. No roots of trees or plants
can live in this permanently frozen ground.

The land looks empty from the air,
but if you travel over it in summer, you find that
it is not really barren and empty at all.
The top layer of soil thaws, and the temperature
of the air sometimes rises to 25°C. There is plenty
of water, and plants can grow.

Victoria Island in July – The snow still lingers along the shore.

As soon as the ground is free of snow, the plants grow quickly, because they must flower and seed before the short summer is over. Millions of flies and mosquitoes breed in the lakes and pools. Thousands of birds fly up from the south to nest and to feed their young on the flies.

A snow bunting has made his nest in one of the tussocks of grass shown in the picture at the top of the page. He is bringing a mosquito to the nestlings who have just hatched.

Two days later, the snow buntings are out of the nest and hopping about. Young birds must grow quickly to be strong enough to fly south when winter comes.

In the picture on the left, a white-crowned sparrow pauses on the way to her nest in the shrub-willow. She has caught a large fly, and is taking it to feed her young.

In sheltered places, you can even find orchids. This lady's slipper orchid was blooming in a patch of low bushes, on the western shore of Hudson Bay. It is only 10 cm high.
In many places, great clumps of flowers, called saxifrage, cover the ground. You can see them on the island in the picture below.

All human beings need some fruit or green food, or they suffer from an illness called scurvy. The plant on the left is called 'scurvy grass'. The first explorers ate it to avoid getting scurvy.

The plant on the right is called 'Labrador tea'. Explorers made a hot drink from its leaves.

There are plenty of fish in the lakes and in the sea, and once the ice has melted, water birds nest in their thousands along the shore.

Many black-throated and red-throated divers, which nest as far south as the northern British Isles, nest in the Arctic. In America, the divers are called 'loons'. The red-throated loon on the left had her nest on a lake.

Arctic tern

Eider duck

Eider duck's nest

Arctic terns nest along the shore. Almost all the birds nesting in the Arctic fly south as soon as the summer has gone. There would be no food for them in the far north, for they cannot fish in a frozen sea. The arctic terns make the longest journey of all. They fly south across the world, right down to the Antarctic. It is summer there, when it is winter in the north.

Eider ducks nest along the coast. If you look back to page 7 you can just see eggs in an eider duck's nest under a rock.

The eider duck plucks out the little feathers from her breast to make a soft nest for her young. The nestlings keep warm in a nest of eider down.

The days are long in summer. On midsummer day along the Arctic circle the sun does not set at all, and the farther north you go, the longer the daylight lasts. But when winter comes, the nights are as long as the summer days.

The animals which live in the Arctic have to adapt to the winter. Caribou (North American reindeer) move south to the shelter of the trees, but they are still in a land of ice and snow. Their coats grow thicker, and their feet change in a remarkable way. In summer, the large soft pads of their feet keep them from sinking in the ground. In winter, their foot pads shrink and hair grows between their toes to cover them. Their hooves grow rapidly. The caribou can then travel on the outer rim of their hooves, and their foot pads do not touch the hard, frozen ground.

Lemming

Lemmings live on the shoots
of young grass. In the autumn
they make nests of dried grass
on top of the ground,
and line them with fur.
When the snow falls,
each lemming tunnels about
under the snow, eating
grass stems and moving from
nest to nest.

Arctic ground squirrels
hibernate. They sleep
for about seven months.
They dig burrows in
the summer, with a den
to one side. They line
the den with grasses and
lichens and caribou fur.
When the cold comes,
they curl up in their dens
and fall deeply asleep
until spring.

*Arctic
ground
squirrel*

Most coyotes live farther
south, among the forests
and on the prairies,
but in the last 150 years,
they have spread northwards.
They live on lemmings,
ground squirrels and foxes.

Coyote

Arctic foxes often make their dens in dry ridges of sand and gravel. They are chocolate brown and cream in summer, but in winter arctic foxes grow a new coat, as white as snow, so that they cannot easily be seen. Both hunters and hunted need to be as invisible as possible, if they are to survive.

Arctic fox

The cubs are grey, but by winter they will be white, too. The young fox cub in the picture below was hungry. He was waiting for his father or mother to return with food. He heard a strange noise, and looked out to see what it was.

There are no trees in
the Arctic, so the birds
nest on the ground,
or in low bushes.
Young birds cannot
escape their enemies,
but, because of the colour
of their feathers,
they are almost invisible
among the mosses
and lichens.

Golden plover chick

Golden plover

The mother golden plover
is watching her chick.
She calls to him
at the approach of danger.
He lies perfectly still.
Only his eyes blink.
When her chicks are
in danger, the mother
pretends to be injured,
so that any animal hunting
for food will follow her,
and not see the chick.

In winter, when plovers
fly south, they are
dull brown and buff.
Some of them fly as
far south as Australia.

*The golden plover
pretending to be injured.*

A ptarmigan on her nest

Some birds stay in the Arctic all the year round.
They need protective colouring, too. In summer,
the ptarmigan looks so like the surrounding plants,
that you may almost step on her before you see her.

Male ptarmigan in summer plumage

In winter, ptarmigan
grow white feathers,
so that it is difficult
to see them against
the snow. The male
ptarmigan has some white
feathers even in summer.
Only the female sits on
the eggs, so it does not
matter quite so much
if the male bird is seen.

Young birds are in danger not only from foxes and other animals, but also from other birds. The ptarmigan in the picture had made her nest very close to that of a long-tailed jaeger. Jaegers sometimes take the eggs and young of other birds for food, so it was very important for the ptarmigan not to be seen.

A long-tailed jaeger looking for food.

Some animals do not change the colour of their coats. Polar bears and arctic wolves are white, for it is more important for them to be hidden in winter, when food is scarce.
Polar bears live along the edge of the arctic ice in winter, and chiefly along the shore in the summer. Polar bears are very good swimmers. In winter they live on seals, which they find on the ice-floes. Their white coats help them to steal up, unnoticed, on their prey.

In summer, the polar bears come to land
to eat berries and mushrooms, and young birds
which they find in the nests along the shore.
They eat lemmings, too, and the carcasses of
whales and dead animals.

The bears wander about alone for most of
the year, but they come together to mate in June.
When winter comes, the female digs a den in the snow,
or in a dry hill. She sleeps through the winter,
and the cubs are born in the den. They stay
with their mother, learning how to hunt food,
until they are nearly two years old.

The male bears only sleep for one or two months
in winter.

Arctic wolves eat small animals, such as
ground squirrels and lemmings, and they also
hunt together in packs, to kill larger animals.
Even a polar bear will retreat if threatened by
a wolf pack.

Arctic wolf

© Robert Bateman-1978-

A wolf kill – The bones of a caribou on the ground

The caribou are an important source of meat
for arctic wolves. They were even more important
for the human beings who first came to the Arctic
to live thousands of years ago. These were
the Eskimos. The name 'Eskimo' was given them
by the Cree Indians, who were their nearest neighbours
to the south. In the Cree language, 'Eskimo' means
'eater of raw meat'. The Eskimos call themselves
the 'Innuit', which is a word in their own language
meaning 'the people'. Small groups of Eskimos
live together, often a long way from other Innuit,
and a group sometimes has a special name of its own.
For example, the Innuit who lived near Coppermine
called themselves the Kilinenuit, which means
'the people on the edge of the land'.

It is only in the last 300 years that
the Eskimos have had contacts with white men,
and until about 150 years ago they lived entirely
by hunting and fishing, and by gathering berries
and plants. They made all their own
weapons and boats and homes and clothes.
They travelled by dogsled in winter, or walked
long distances in search of food.

The caribou was a very important animal for them.
They ate caribou meat. During the summer,
they lived in skin tents, made of caribou hide,
and they used caribou skins to make warm clothes
to keep out the terrible winter cold. The Innuit
wore trousers made of caribou skins, and on top of
these went a 'parka', a kind of fur anorak,
made of two layers of skins. The top skin has
the fur on the outside, and the underskin has
the fur on the inside. The fur traps a layer of
warm air next to the skin, and a parka is the warmest,
lightest garment you can wear. The parka reaches
down nearly to the knees, and a warm fur hood is
part of it.

When they travelled in winter, the Eskimos made
their homes from blocks of snow. The houses were
called 'igloos'. An Eskimo family could travel freely
in both summer and winter, hunting animals
and gathering food when the weather was fine.
In summer, they lived in their skin tents.
In winter, they could build an igloo in a few hours,
wherever they decided to camp.

The ring of stones in the picture once held down
the edge of an Eskimo tent. The pile of stones
on the left was a 'cache', containing the bones of
a seal an Eskimo had killed. Stones were piled over
the dead seal so that wild animals could not take it.

Today, you will find very few Eskimos following
the old way of life, but you can see how they once
lived from the carvings they have made.

The carving below is made of ivory, from
walrus' tusks. It shows an igloo, with a sledge
and a dog team outside. The sledge is turned
upside down, because it is so cold that the runners
would freeze to the ground if it were left overnight.
The igloo has two 'rooms'. The smaller room acts as
a passageway, so that the cold wind doesn't blow
straight into the larger room where the family lives.

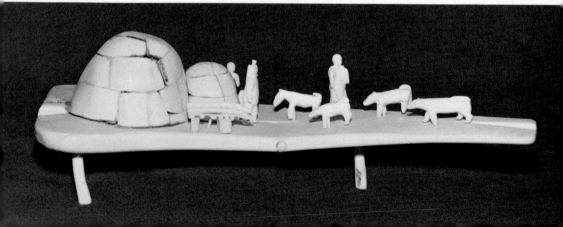

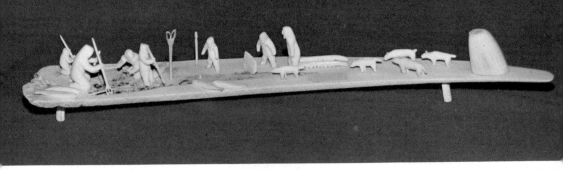

In this carving, the Eskimos are fishing.
In summer, they fish in the sea and the lakes
and rivers, and dry some of the fish in the sun,
to use in winter. In winter, they fish
through a hole in the ice. They also catch seals.
Seals have to come up out of the water to breathe,
and when the sea is covered with ice, the seal keeps
a small hole open. A man will often stand for hours
by a seal hole, waiting with his spear ready.

Seals were very important to the Eskimos
who lived along the coast. They provided food,
oil for their lamps, and skins for waterproof boots.

The carving below shows a woman fishing in a lake,
while two men are hunting a muskox. You can see
caribou passing on the far side of the lake.

A muskox is much bigger than a caribou.
Muskox have great, heavy horns, and a very
thick coat to keep out the winter cold.

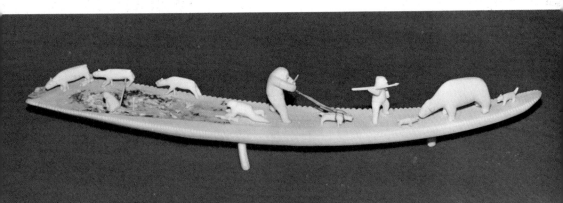

This carving shows
an Eskimo woman who is
just going to have a baby.
Other women have come
to help her. One stands
behind her, holding her
firmly. The two women
sitting in front will take
the baby when it comes,
and then give it to
the mother to care for.

An Eskimo mother carries
her baby on her back
in a kind of bag, which is
slung over her shoulders.
The baby is kept warm
even in the winter cold
by the heat from his
mother's body.

He is kept dry and clean
by putting handfuls of
a light, dry moss on
the bottom of the bag.
The moss can be changed
whenever it is necessary.
There is plenty of moss
in the Arctic.

This is a model of a kayak made by an Eskimo

Kayaks are made by stretching scraped skins over a light wooden frame. A kayak is so light, that it can easily be carried by one man. The Eskimos used kayaks for fishing, and for hunting seals and walrus. Caribou often take to the water to escape their enemies.

The stone bird on the kayak can be moved from side to side to balance the boat. A spear is attached to a float, so that the hunter can recover his catch when he spears a fish.

Bright sunlight on the snow can damage your eyes, causing snow-blindness. So the Eskimos made themselves bone eye shades with slits which only let in a little light.

Eskimo eye shade

23

Eskimo children used to learn everything from
their parents. The boys learned how to hunt
and catch fish, how to drive a dog team and
build an igloo, and how to find their way across
the great, wild country in which they lived.
The girls learned how to make clothes out of skins
for all the family, how to prepare food and
how to take care of the children. They learned
how to keep the lamp alight through the long,
dark nights of the winter.

The lamp, which was made of stone, belonged to
the wife in an Eskimo family. It was like a small,
deep, narrow dish, and it had a wick made of moss.
For fuel, the Eskimos used blubber. (Blubber is
the fat from a seal.) The lamp gave the Eskimos
light and warmth.

In the evenings, the older people told the children
stories and legends of the past.

An Eskimo girl today

But in the last 100 years, and especially
in the last 50 years, there have been great changes
in the way in which the Eskimos live.

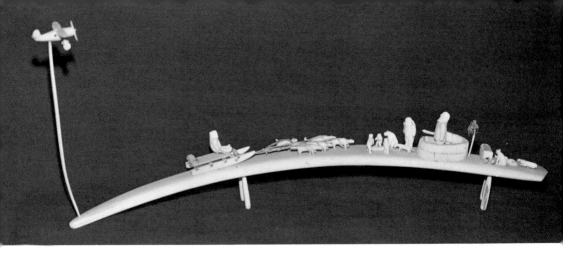

In this carving, an Eskimo is building an igloo.
He is looking up, astonished to see an aeroplane.

Eskimos had been in contact with the outside world
for a long time before the first aeroplane came.
They had met white men who traded in furs.

In 1670, the King of England granted a charter to
'The Governor and Company of Adventurers of England
trading into Hudson's Bay'. By this charter,
the Hudson's Bay Company was made 'true and absolute
Lords and Proprietors' of nearly two million square
kilometres of the Canadian North. Animals that live in
the far north have coats of thick fur in winter.
These could be sold in Europe for a good price.
People wanted them for clothes, and fur was in fashion.

The traders went first to the Indians who lived
farther south. But as they travelled across the country,
they met groups of Eskimos. Trading posts were set up.
The traders offered the Indians and Eskimos all kinds
of goods in exchange for the animals' furs. The Eskimos
wanted the strangers' rifles, knives, pots and pans.
They could kill caribou more easily with a rifle than
a spear. These goods would make their lives easier.

The Eskimos began to spend less time hunting for their own needs, and more time trapping animals for the fur trade. They travelled less in winter, because they had to stay near their trap lines. So their way of life slowly began to change.

But it was the coming of the aeroplane which made possible the rapid changes which have taken place in the last 50 years. Until then, travel was slow and difficult. But sea-planes can land on lakes in the summer. In winter they can be fitted with skis and land on the snow.

It is easy to fly to the Canadian Arctic now. Hunters go there to shoot animals. Prospectors go there looking for gold, copper, uranium and other minerals. Oil and natural gas have both been found in the Arctic.

The picture shows an Eskimo settlement at Bathurst Inlet, on the northern coast of Canada as it is today. It is close to a naturalists' lodge, where people who are interested in wildlife stay. Twenty years ago, the lodge was a trading post of the Hudson's Bay Company.

The Eskimos who live in Bathurst Inlet have been
among the last to give up their old way of life,
but even their life is changing rapidly now.

As you can see in the picture on page 26,
their houses are made of aluminium. They are
much warmer and drier than igloos or skin tents.
These Eskimos follow many of the old ways
of their people. They catch and dry fish
during the summer. You can see the fish being dried
in the sun in the picture. They hunt caribou for a
supply of meat through the winter. (The two boys
in the picture on page 1 live here.) The men work
as guides during the two months of summer,
and the women help in the lodge. In this way,
they earn money to buy many things they need.

When they go out to
hunt caribou, they look
for them with binoculars.
They use rifles, and
they no longer travel
in kayaks. They use boats
with outboard motors,
and they wear modern
Canadian clothes.

*One of the Eskimos
in Bathurst Inlet
steering his boat.*

Some Eskimos still use sledges pulled by dog teams when they travel in winter.

But many of them use snowmobiles instead of dogs. Snowmobiles have skis and motors to drive them over the snow.

Snowmobile and sledge

There are today between 10,000 and 15,000 Eskimos in Canada. When they lived by hunting and fishing, they used to travel in small family groups, but now they live in small 'settlements', scattered through the Arctic. (You might call them large villages or small towns.) You find them along the northern coast, or in the 'barren lands' north of the tree line, or on some of the northern islands, or along the shores of Hudson Bay.

They live together in larger groups today, so that the Canadian Government can provide them with modern houses, doctors, hospitals and schools. Nowadays, Eskimo children go to school like other children, and learn to live in the modern world.

But Canada is an immense country. If you live in England, you are closer to someone living on the east coast of Canada, than that person is to someone living on the Canadian west coast. One Eskimo settlement is often still hundreds of kilometres from the next, and even farther from the big cities of the south.

Nowadays, some Eskimo women go out to work. The women in the picture above work in a fish factory on Victoria Island. Arctic char (fish rather like salmon) are caught in the sea there. They are cleaned and packed in the factory, and then sent to the cities in the far south.

Eskimo women have always decorated the clothes they made for their families, by using fur of different colours.

When the big town centre, called 'the complex', was built in Churchill on Hudson Bay, the Eskimos made the bright-coloured cloth banners which you can see in the picture.

For thousands of years, the Eskimo people
made their own fish-hooks, spearheads and tools
from the bones of animals they had killed,
or from stone. In the dark winter months,
they sometimes carved pieces of stone,
or ivory walrus' tusks.

Today, carving is one of the ways in which Eskimos
can earn money. Their carvings are sold in the shops
in the south. Then they can buy food and clothes,
rifles and fishing gear, in the local Hudson's Bay
Company's store.

Life is changing in the Arctic for the animals, too.
The great herds of caribou are much smaller than
they used to be. No one is quite sure why this is,
but it is much easier to kill caribou with rifles
than with spears, and perhaps too many have been killed.
Hunters from the south can fly up to the north by 'plane.
In the past 50 years, so many polar bears have been shot
that people were afraid that one day there would be
no polar bears left at all.

There are many more people from the south living
in the Arctic now. Some of them are miners
and prospectors. Some are drilling for oil and
natural gas. Oil and gas have both been found in
the far north, and they have to be sent to the cities
of the south through long pipelines, laid above ground.

Once, enemies of North America had to cross the ocean
in ships to get there. But now aeroplanes and rockets
could be used to attack across the North Pole.
So an early warning system, called the 'Dew Line',
has been built in the far north.

Part of the Dew Line on Victoria Island

There is a launching site near Churchill
for rockets which send up satellites. If you look
back to the picture on page 6, you can see
the launching area. The satellites are tracked by radar.
The picture below shows the radar tracking station.

All the changes taking place in the Arctic affect not only the people, but also every creature there. Biologists are studying the birds and mammals, to find out how they live, in order to protect them.

The biologist in the picture is studying eider ducks. He is weighing one of the chicks. It doesn't hurt the chick, and it is put back in the nest.

There are plans to set aside large tracts of land where the animals and plants will be able to go on living undisturbed. The animals need protection if they are to survive. Hunters are no longer allowed to kill polar bears. The bears still wander, as they have done for thousands of years, along the edge of the frozen sea.